D1447197

8th House Publishing
Montreal, Canada

Copyright © 8th House Publishing 2022
First Edition

All rights reserved under International and Pan-American Copyright
Conventions. No part of this book may be reproduced in any form or by any
electronic or mechanical means, including information storage and retrieval
systems, without permission in writing from the publisher, except by a
reviewer, who may quote brief passages in a review.

Published worldwide by 8th House Publishing.
Illustrations & Cover Design by Rolli

ISBN 978-1-926716-63-3

Designed by 8th House Publishing.
www.8thHousePublishing.com
Set in Garamond, Raleway & Grobold.

LIBRARY AND ARCHIVES CANADA CATALOGUING IN PUBLICATION

Title: Plumstuff : poems & drawings / Rolli.
Other titles: Plum stuff
Names: Rolli, author.
Description: Previously published under title: Plum stuff. Montreal, Canada:
8th House Publishing,
   2010. | Includes index.
Identifiers: Canadiana 20220162891 | ISBN 9781926716633 (softcover)
Classification: LCC PS8635.O4465 P58 2022 | DDC C811/.6—dc23

PLUMSTUFF

poems & drawings

Rolli

also by Rolli

The Sea-Wave
Mavor's Bones

for children

Kabungo

CONTENTS

Note

for Claire

NOTE

Warty, immature, under-edited. First books are, at the best of times, all of these things. My debut title, *Plum Stuff*, was no exception. Instead of letting oblivion devour the book whole, though, its publisher has graciously permitted me to revise the text, lance its warts, dress it up with fresh drawings—and insert some new poems, too. It's a dream opportunity, and I'm grateful to 8th House for providing it.

Plum Stuff is now *Plumstuff*—and ripe, at last. I hope you enjoy its flavours.

—*Rolli*

PLUMSTUFF

poems & drawings

I. LiTeRaTe

If ever I write a book

so bland
it's championed
by every
living
critic

      seize
      my pen

and bash me
compassionately
until

I'm still

The Muse

Surprised
to find her thickish in
sandals and robe
holding midlife like
a yelping whelp
he approached her
the poet
discreetly

You're not quite lovely he
said
in some gentle way

You came merely to see? the
answer

And be inspired

Sighing
Shut your eyes

Surprised
to find she'd struck him
with a thickish limb
the poet reproached her
(from a judicious
distance)

Interrupting—

If you think it's
a lapdog business
lolling on pillows till
my breath stirs your
pen
think again

I stalk women
and men
prone to idleness (poets)
and goad them in my style—no
gentle one

You will know I've struck
when you wake
from the blood on
the walls—off
you go

Which he did
insensible
swift

I too

can be a poet

I too
can sit inconspicuous in
an obvious café

cosmopolitan
cockroach

antennae brushed
back

black beret

From *How to Compose a Poem, Volume II*

Now your navel's
smell
detail
as prosaically
as possible

If are akin
your words
to nothing in
magazines

hurriedly
burn
the page

*Averageness is
the caviar
of the Plastic
Age*

The golden ball

One evening
fell
on my dreaming
skull

the golden ball

      a gorgeous
      metaphor

Morning
opening
my eyes

      I could not
      recall it

There have been
many metaphors
yes
in my consciousness

   yet held
   next
   that only
   golden
   one

everything else
is just
dust

Aunt Gray and Octavius and I

of a Sunday
pond-squatting watch
the poets float
by
throw them crusts and such

(and the way they
peck themselves
fetching blood—wonderful
for children)

clap! clap! clap! clap!

Our new tactic's picking a single
ducky
tossing him all
the crusts one week—then we
leap in and he feeds
us

Rinse and repeat!

What other poets?

Oh they float more often
it seems
feet in the air
heads unseen
       some fashion
       I imagine
              the new humor—you
              know poets

Ta-ta!

Wave
Octavius
Wave!

Can you say
lucky ducky?

As incongruous as

a poet in
a mansion

       imagination

in this tanned and
flexing
century

When robots poems compose

dab canvasses and
brilliantly
sing

will we clasp
at last hands
humanity as

we stroll grimly in-
to the ocean?

The Mystery Mind

The British Mystery Mind
in all her *parlour room glory*
hopped from one to the next lap
sloshing tea
tossing autographed copies
of her newest (*Nude Dagger*)
hot off a press so hot they leaped like she did
one to one
startled frogs

Really whispered Mini Jane
into the ear of Chastity Sedgewick Mercury
May Crane
what can one say of a woman unwed
squeezing midlife like
          a shipwrecker's barrel in the sea
          a pinchpenny's toothpaste tube
with a braid—trailing—down
to her DERRIÈRE?

Such awful hair
muttered Chastity
smilingly
as the Mystery Mind
dropped onto her (laughing) lap

O critic stick

in my throat
the thorned
rose

This soft
vase
honor

Odium/glory
yours

From the acid red fruit

by those grown
who cannot stand
a man to see
succeeding

> harvested with
> hard jaws
> and squeezed
> like a beating
> heart

I have composed the most
refreshing
beverage

which I nightly
imbibe

with more joy than
you can
imagine

My bankbook looking in will

I an ode
compose
to a gorgeous
Roman
jar

or

at an ashen
cashier
flash
my pilfered
pistol?

Fell down well—send

book
and candle and
vanish

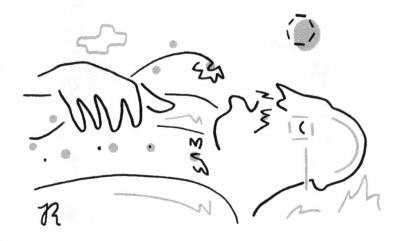

II. PHiLoSoPHiCaL

Myth of Manhattan

Adream she
wrote poems

tossed them on
water
and watched them
oddly
ossify

      colossal
      flute-bones
      floating

She breathed
and through bone
holes rose
in columns a solid
city
singing

      Then she set
      down her pen

      yes

      and rode water
      crests west

I am sorry so

madames and
messieurs
to learn
of your condition

To be twisted
as willows with
indignation

   misérable

Know though
swallowing
these capsules will
cure your
disorder

for each holds
one crumb
of the only
à propos
medicine

   a sense of humor

Fascism

Until the day
we can speak
what we please

        all to all
        sans dam-
        nation

and pen any-
thing
and sing

children

        there can be
        no democracy

Be calm—all

we need
humanity

to grease these
frictions is

a simple one
million
years

of evolution

Pick a side kindly

so we know

to float you
on our
shoulders

or

scrimshaw
your ribs
with pitch-
forks

and none judge
by
their character
for

the twentieth
century's
dead

We flew all farther apart

as the stars

and stand as
mountains
scowling
over seas

at nemeses we
cannot
remember

Though no one's swung

by anyone's
opinion

the redundant
tongue
worms on

(perversion)

1. Open your skull

2. All
the dark colonies
of your brain-
cave
shake
away

3. Wait
in ignorant
enlightenment

for your first
autonomous
thought

If you're so morose

(said the medic
to the Supreme Being)

that you man-
ufactured man
(wretched jesters)
to hearten
your heart

I'll prescribe
this instant

the most god-
strong omni-
potent
pills

Hymn of the puritans

There are only
below
one's clothes more
clothes

and under
those
more and more

For we're all
matryoshka
dolls
and our souls

are atoms in
flowering
gowns

The faintly-coloured English

London

the thickness of it
fog
like umber yesterday's gravy

its cross-stitch of people
        the church
        and the steeple
nogging their heads on the baulks

It's simple to feel
you've stuck your finger in
Britannica and slammed it
shut

(your finger
then your elbow
belly and so
on dropping
clothes as you go)

So I'm glutted with
loco *hey ho*
wind and rain

For the wind's windy
as Church in a fray
rain reigny as old Victoria
glowering roses shut at sun-
down
taut as her donjon thighs

Now Switzerland's bright and beige
a poem on a page
white margins and wide

It's been ages

Bye-bye

Laughed the capitalist

To a boulder roll
of stuff up
the summit's
the life my
children

(Sing along)

For a moment don't
rest and never
glance
down

Life climbs the staircase

lays dollar
on top
step

watches
you
bend
then

lends boot to
your
posterior

More sense self-

pity to pity

ones sighing
in green gardens than

dim prisons singing
freely
of green

The condemned man

Select
they said
the method

and the condemned
man's last
words were

Please
the guillotine

kneeling
appreciative of
the democracy
of options

as the cold
blade
lowered

If it pleases you

to believe
of me
prooflessly
a rumor

who am I
with cruel
truth

to purloin
your only
joy?

Man/dandy

[On a lawn.]

MAN: What's that—druthering?

DANDY: Druthering?

MAN: Yes. The noise wind makes when it's—druthering.

[A faint druthering sound.]

MAN: There it is again!

DANDY: I'm sure it's nothing.

MAN: Maybe. You were saying?

DANDY: Hmm? Right. Ideas. Dried up. Completely. All we ever did, once, was fish them from the reeds with bare fingers, thick and fat and easy. And when they dove lower, looked lower, sweated and profited. Then patience, waiting, toss-backs, distraction. Then stillness. Extinction. Or think of it … as a smashed egg.

MAN: And all the king's horses and all the king's men...

DANDY: Have long since given up, ghosts and all. A millennium of letters, of patching the egg, and every method's tested, reechoed, dead. There's an end to creation, as there's an end to the universe.

MAN: That could easily be, yes. Or you might just be incredibly lazy.

[More druthering. Louder, this time.]

MAN: Are you sure you don't hear it?

DANDY: Hear what?

MAN: The druthering.

DANDY: Well, of course I hear it.

MAN: And it doesn't concern you?

DANDY: *[Waving, dismissive.]* We're mere years from Cement Death, when no idea, mishmash, hash—no *action*, even—can be.

MAN: And what then?

DANDY: Everything. *Nothing.* Industry, people, our very machineries will freeze. We'll stiffen in place, monuments to mediocrity, strike poses, hold them forever. I've picked mine already. *[He rises, extends his limbs like wings of a bird of prey.]* What do you think?

[Druthering—very loud and close.]

MAN: *[Wide-eyed.]* Did you hear that? Behind us.

DANDY: I couldn't turn, now, if I wanted to.

[A rustling in the hedge, and out springs—a lion. MAN and DANDY run off together. The lion grins, slinks back into the hedge. And that's that.]

Make me mediocre so

I at last can cram

into skin stitched
for me

by society

If in this dreaming city

we can scrawl
our futures

let's sketch
together
steps

and crawl
to the stars

III. BeWiTCHiNG

On the brim standing

of the still river

> such mute
> beauty

my soul stepped in
and out
of its mansion

> again and
> again

as a summer cat

The lady with the cream long cigarettes

budding from her fingertips
drew one
another—plus
young men wondering
where she got them
when

and it was time only before
out slipped both cigarette and
some profundity

Language evolved

> *gesture*
> *alphabet*
> *cigarette*

Words are obsolete

We clumped about her
sputtering
sucking in
loving the cream long things
slid so elegantly in
and out
and in

(The mole on her neck proved distracting
drawing one's eyes
as it did
from the mole on her chin)

Styles Andrew

-lay in a chaise lounge
(when standing even)
slick and cool
as liquor in the vein

(to put up a column/wall
was to see him leaning
appear
lit cig in finger)

-encrypted his skin in
January tans
unwrinkled as if
by itch/whim

-hapless had
a lord's home—or
its summer run
(winter a mystery)

-was Finnish/Dutch/such
a race

-specifically lived
        all over the place

Ethics is

a sweater
that itches

ditch
it
skinny-
dip

I am a Persian cat

Today
I am a Persian cat

Cat's menu du jour do
not a thing
          excepting perhaps nap

I will clean my fur
most certainly
some

in alley sing
to clean
my lung

fa mi
          do mi
mi do

then go
sit in windows so
the moon knows
how glowing to be
(seeing me)

We

in that green
museum
of our frailties

     the modern park

on the pond-
bridge pausing saw
floating

below no
flyblown
bodies

nor above one
opiated
angel

The pine-
shadow cowled
not one
clandestine
man

     So we yawned and
     wandered
     home

Jo-Ann?

The last I saw her
sporting the faux élan of the day
like a stolen wristwatch
we talked a little (little
to address—a dress
I'd fit in minced)
shammed laughter and
bolted for polar doors

God! When we're on
our knees
he's rallying back
to these
unfeeling
our returns

> Her bones show *so*
> they'd be simple to pick

Her son's a bum
husband inebriate/thick

Breathe critically!

The Anglo-Indian widow

wore weeds chic
as an imperial lawn—on
a mystic-slim income

Apart from crunching lump-
sugar (and publishing verse)
she had no vices—but one night
skimmed off with a coffee-
skinned milkman

In a straw hut on
a jungle plantation
they squat very simply still
it's said

But a good woman
too

Usually so level-headed

The girl in the umbrella

looked good to me
        not that I could see
but her feet
but still
she looked good to me

Sandee—she
lands this week

From the station
to Immigration
        then out for steak

It's not too rush-rush Mum
for me

Just us
the Justice
the porter
the hotel doors
the bed

        then

opening the umbrella
at last

Oh queen we rose so only

we
behind thee might see
the celebrity

The girl who writes about stars

I

There's the *Girl Who Writes About Stars*
praised to the same heights

You might find her
of an evening
between Cetus
and Chameleon
blinking
on the end of a string

Far below
the *Man in Green*
with his brass telescope

The *Blush Mum*—one
hand gripping the string-
end and one
throwing coins
to men with bellows
(*Bellowsmen*)
who squeezing keep
the girl afloat

A *Man with a Pipe* arrives

If we're not cautious
says the Man in Green
folding his telescope
a play might break out
any minute

II

BLUSH MUM: [*Fondly. Looking up.*] My daughter, sir.

MAN IN GREEN: I see.

BLUSH MUM: Talent rises. Genius flies.

MAN IN GREEN: [*Sighing.*] So it seems.

GIRL WHO WRITES ABOUT STARS: A star, a star is a smudge. A smudge, a smudge…

MAN WITH PIPE: [*Leaning in.*] Might I relieve you, missus?

BLUSH MUM: [*Severely.*] No. Thank you.

MAN WITH PIPE: Well, I will anyways—I'm *not* married. Har!

BLUSH MUM: I don't understand.

MAN WITH PIPE: Humourless, I see. Tell me— are you the twenty-first century?

BLUSH MUM: Go away!

GIRL WHO WRITES ABOUT STARS: The moon, the moon is a bruise. A bruise, a bruise…

MAN IN GREEN: Sir? Backwards to ask, but … are you Irish, or a pirate?

MAN WITH PIPE: [*Ignoring him.*] Kiss me, missus. [*Taking her hand.*]

BLUSH MUM: I won't stand for this, sir!

MAN WITH PIPE: We can lie, if you like. [*She swats him with her non-string hand.*] Kiss me, missus. Kiss me.

BLUSH MUM: [*To the Man in Green (who's begun pitching stones at the Girl Who Writes About Stars) while synchronously swatting the Man with Pipe.*] What are you doing?

MAN IN GREEN: Throwing stones. I can't bear the sight of her.

BLUSH MUM: No! She's ethereal! She's a gemstone! Amethyst! Don't you dare!

MAN IN GREEN: If she doesn't like it [*throwing*], she can jolly well fly away, can't she?

GIRL WHO WRITES ABOUT STARS: The stars, the stars are bruises. Bruises, bruises…

BLUSH MUM: [*Nervously.*] I suppose.

MAN IN GREN: [*Throwing another stone*]. Indeed.

GIRL WHO WRITES ABOUT STARS: My face is bruised. My arms … are smudged…

BLUSH MUM: [*Whispering.*] Stop it! Alright. *You* know—*I* know—she can't actually fly. It's the Bellowsmen who keep her afloat, and only because I pay them. *They* don't love her.

BELLOWSMEN: [*Together, puffing away.*] Certainly not!

MAN IN GREEN: Why don't you tell *her* that? And stop this disgusting charade?

BLUSH MUM: Now? After all these years? She'd *die*! And *that* would spell catastrophe—for us all!

MAN IN GREEN: P-I-G-S-H-I-T. Nothing like it. [*Throwing stones.*]

BELLOWSMEN: [*Sitting.*] Time for a rest!

BLUSH MUM: Wait! Do you have to?

BELLOWSMEN: Well ... you got any more coins, ma'am?

BLUSH MUM: [*Checking her pocket.*] None! But please—I promise, I'll—oh, just don't let her fall!

BELLOWSMEN: Too late.

GIRL WHO WRITES ABOUT STARS: Smuuudge...

MAN WITH PIPE: Kiss me, kiss me, kiss...

GIRL WHO WRITES ABOUT STARS: Bruuuise...

BELLOWSMEN: Break's over.

MAN IN GREEN: [*Throwing stones at the Bellowsmen.*] Not so much.

BELLOWSMEN: Hey! We can't work like this. Un-union!

BLUSH MUM: [*Letting go of the string, running back and forth, arms out.*] I'll catch you, I'll catch you!

BELLOWSMEN: Dear! Looks like the whole damn sky's coming down with her! Like in a picture book. Rich!

BLUSH MUM: [*To the Man in Green, shrieking.*] I *told* you this would happen!

III

KABOOM!

(Blinking)

So I will
as cat on pill-
ow or-
igami me
to sleep

IV. EPiCuReaN

You are a *peach* of a man

-in the belly especially
the bum (plump
and fuzzed)

-in the eyes
the sun colour of
a pippin winter sun

-and the smell
gentle of milk
and potted something green

> There's nothing so quenching
> it's said
> as peach juice

> There's nothing so fine
> as the meat
> of the peach

A good idea

is one among
a million
common
bottles

wedged
in cellars
of mind

some spent
cognoscente
sighing
finally
finds

The Swiss thin immigrant

shrinking in a wash of coffee
touched nothing but
the odd square caramel (and hairy
Bulgarian men)

Distressing—yet we said
nothing
knowing it would only
snip the wrong wire
and blow us
to the tip of liberty's pointy iron tiara

Her mother died
of the selfsame thin
in addition to cigarettes

Vexed at the end—*an effect*
said the doc
of brain starvation
weighing no more than those
odd square caramels
we'd watched her pop
go boa-like down her throat

Tomorrow?

Grocery shopping

I'm an olive

in gin

It's a pleasure
to swim

(pim-
ento)

Friday night

I was drunk on
sauvignon

writing
triolets

my note-
pad slanting
to catch
the lamp-
light

> For a moment
> closing
> my eyes

I woke
as the dawn
was putting on
its clothes

The moon is an alcoholic

floating home in
the bottle-
dark
morning

V. FaTaL

When fell at last the last poets

among
the golden
leaves

we combed them
in-
to black bags
weeping

and weeping

Casually drowned

In the easy same way he did everything
   eat a plum
   pluck a string
trip into an inheritance or
the arms of a bathing bachelorette heiress
(this happened on various occasions)
he stepped out with the sea
one evening

We felt nor grief nor affection
according to fashion

Though we each of us miss his—insouciance?
Is this the word?

We miss his insouciance

His mistress has his insurance

   but misses his insouciance too

Nothing on TV

so we slayed
old Halloway

his reputation
raped

(laughing) and

him lifted
willing in-
to the noose

>   the stool
>   kicked
>   free

then went
to a movie

Plop-bauble

All's I know inspectors there
was a plop-bauble
an' a clink-trinket
          then the lights come on again an'
bofe of 'em's dead

Dad at the window
gagged with sashes—a
rose in 'is throat
an' the broken vase on 'is lap

An' Mum—plum from
a twisted napkin
blops o' sherry tearin'
down 'er chin

S'ppose it do move me
up queue for their
FORTUNE O' MILLIONS

But—you can't suspicion *me*?

Serious?

Larf!

So light the day

as a halved
apple that

> for seconds for-
> getting

> our servitude to
> the super-
> computers

we practically
laughed

The stone throwers

before
more stones throwing
know
the stone throwers

will come
to crush one
gorgeous day *your*
brains

and will wish
you *Why*

       collapsing
       hit

did I not toss
helmets?

Shall we stroll

the tall-
grassed
middle
path

to a promontory

unfold
our golden
telescopes
then

observe
the world
burn?

Pardon the interruption—but

you must something other
wish
to accomplish
with your mortal
clay

than kiln it in-
to a skeleton
whitening beneath
this inscription:

He had a flat abdomen

???

Our sweet deity called him

gently and he stepped
from grass
to avenue

and the liquor
truck struck
him

and his blessed
head
as a cannon-
ball shot

angelically
to heaven

Ra-tom wakes in the afterlife

The last he recalled
a jackal had him by the tail

To one who slept on softness this
was beastly effrontery

But the dog was gone
and Ra-Tom found himself
in a dusty unlit place

In wraps no less—yet
easily chewed through these

There were rats in bad states
loaves like bones to eat
and seven dry bowls

What place was this?

> No combs nor
> combers
> palm to scratch
> no water
> fire
> no ash

Yet safe from jackal-
dogs and off in corners
stacked-up softness

Dropping on the last
Ra-Tom licked himself
blinking

*

In his dream
he took Anubis by the scruff

and sloughed him in a quarry

The connoisseur

He fell among thorns
then rose

>   over the garden
>   the town

As the world glowed below

Death
he said
is better than expected

The moon's
a cool
moscato and

the sun
a sauvignon

Some stars
he thought
were finer
and nebulae better
as he sampled the universe

For a connoisseur
dessert
eternal

savoring forever

I lighting on

the tomb
of the last known
poet

in tears tore
the weeds
free

re-posed
the cracked
plastic
roses

and rode
home
choking

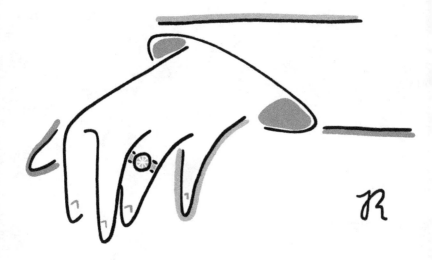

ACKNOWLEDGMENTS

The frontispiece and backispiece drawings first appeared in *Transition*.

The drawing on page 3 first appeared in *The Feathertale Review*.

The drawing on page 45 first appeared in *The Saturday Evening Post*.

The drawing on page 63 first appeared in *The Wall Street Journal*.

The drawings on pages 71 and 87 first appeared in *The Walrus*.

"Oh queen we rose so only" first appeared in *Rattle*.

"The Swiss thin immigrant" first appeared in *Quarterly West*.

"You are a peach of a man" and "Aunt Gray and Octavius and I" first appeared in *The New Quarterly*.

"I too," "The mystery mind" and "Life climbs the staircase" first appeared in *The Feathertale Review*.

"Myth of Manhattan" first appeared in *The Antigonish Review*.

"Plop-bauble" first appeared in *Barnwood*.

"Casually drowned" first appeared in *The Wascana Review*.

ABOUT THE AUTHOR

ROLLI is a Canadian author, cartoonist and songwriter. He's the author of many acclaimed books for adults and children, including *Kabungo* and *The Sea-Wave*. Rolli's stories, poems, drawings and essays are staples of *The New York Times*, *The Saturday Evening Post*, *Playboy*, *The Wall Street Journal*, *Reader's Digest*, *The Walrus*, *Rattle* and other top outlets. Visit Rolli's website (rollistuff.com) and follow him on Twitter at @rolliwrites.

CPSIA information can be obtained
at www.ICGtesting.com
Printed in the USA
LVHW040039290422
717483LV00008B/1378